Turning Over the Earth

Turning Over the Earth

Ralph Black

MILKWEED EDITIONS

Published 2000 by Milkweed Editions
Printed in the United States of America
Cover design by Gail Wallinga
Cover art by Barbara Harman
Interior design by Wendy Holdman
The text of this book is set in Bembo.
00 01 02 03 04   5 4 3 2 1
First Edition

Milkweed Editions, a nonprofit publisher, gratefully acknowledges support from
the Elmer L. and Eleanor J. Andersen Foundation; James Ford Bell Foundation; Bush
Foundation; General Mills Foundation; Honeywell Foundation; Jerome Foundation;
McKnight Foundation; Minnesota State Arts Board through an appropriation by
the Minnesota State Legislature; Norwest Foundation on behalf of Norwest Bank
Minnesota; Lawrence and Elizabeth Ann O'Shaughnessy Charitable Income Trust
in honor of Lawrence M. O'Shaughnessy; Oswald Family Foundation; Ritz Founda-
tion on behalf of Mr. and Mrs. E. J. Phelps Jr.; John and Beverly Rollwagen Fund of
the Minneapolis Foundation; St. Paul Companies, Inc.; Star Tribune Foundation;
Target Foundation on behalf of Dayton's, Mervyn's California and Target Stores;
U.S. Bancorp Piper Jaffray Foundation on behalf of U.S. Bancorp Piper Jaffray; and
generous individuals.

Library of Congress Cataloging-in-Publication Data

Black, Ralph, 1960–
    Turning over the earth / Ralph Black.— 1st ed.
        p. cm.
    ISBN 1-57131-411-3 (pbk.)
        I. Title.

PS3552.L34132 T8 2000
811'.54—dc21   99-088540

This book is printed on acid-free paper.

For my father, *in memoriam;*
and for my mother,
more music than I know

Turning Over the Earth

Don't be surprised we don't know how to describe the world
and only speak of things affectionately by their first names.

—ZBIGNIEW HERBERT

Turning Over the Earth

One

The Muses of Farewell

Suppose when you least expect it
it begins to snow. And suppose
when you are thinking about something
else—the place you meant to visit,
what you meant to say to someone—
the snow continues to fall.
Suppose it keeps falling until
all the roofs of the houses, and all
the parked cars, and all the
streets they are parked on, and
the square in the center of town
are covered. Suppose while you are
sitting in your blue chair
listening to Brahms and scratching
the hair on your arm in a kind of
deliberate, Brahmsian way
inches sift down through the trees.
Then feet. Then drifts begin
to erase the topography of the particular
world you knew so recently so well.
And when you go to the window
to check on the afternoon, there is
nothing but the cold pallor of snow.
And the front door will not open
when you push, and the phone
buzzes an indecipherable noise.
Suppose when you panic and reach
for the fireplace poker and take a swing
at the white beveled glass in the study
snow rolls into the room and fills it,

then fills another, backing you back
toward the back end of the house.
Suppose, then, when you open your mouth
to make that final, almost
human cry—because there is nothing left
but this—no noise comes out, only
silence and snow. And suppose, at last,
that the last thing you think of
as the snow overtakes you in the kitchen
and your blood starts to slow, and
your marrow to freeze, and
the gel of your eyes to thicken—
is Kafka walking the streets of Prague
in the middle of some dismal February night,
his thin face cinched against the
edged Czechoslovakian wind.
And though you know what he knows
can save you, some half-uttered
sentence, some gesture or look,
his pace only quickens in the gathering
cold. For he knows the terror
of the terror of belief, the sorrow
of metaphor, the impossibility of parable
to make the world into anything else.
So you are left at the end to the
muses of snow, who are the muses of
seduction, who are the muses of farewell
and this roomful of weather you have
nuanced, like all of us, out of your life.

Toward a Theory of Harmonics

At the instant one of the last
apples on the winter-ravaged tree
unhinges itself and drops,
heavy with earth-weariness,
a waxwing on the same branch
of the same tree presses both wings
against the air and lifts,
so that the flight and the falling
resonate into the world,
leaving balance tactile, intact.

At the instant the solitary *cronk*
of a south-cruising Canada goose
unflaps itself out of the cold
and launches its cry over these
thousand acres, a single oak leaf
reaches its perfect rust-colored pitch
and rises into lightness. And the silence
its rising and pitch is made of
meets and transposes the kingdom-
making note of the disappearing bird.

And I can't help but think
of the night my father's heart caved in,
the cry of his clutching and the quiet
that clutching met and became.
That I woke that hour, returning to
the very consciousness he left, seems right,
though it's only now I wonder
what woke me: his life or his lifelessness,
his departing-from or moving-toward.

It is like the note a cello makes
when the bow is almost purred
across the strings, balanced exactly
between touching and not-touching.
Or even the shudder of bodies, tuned
and delirious in the pitch of sex.
Some say of the stones that they hold inside
a measure of the earth's first noise.
I lift one heavy with song and vanishing
and I heave it into the weeds.

The Creatures of Home

And so, and so. And so it is
the day before my mother turns
the age of her own old age, small
wren-body, eyes creased with light,
she calls to mark the dailiness,
the weather of days laced in sand,
the light of an hour winnowed through
whatever heaven is. She calls
to talk of groceries to buy, plants
for the garden in spring, fuses
that need changing. Behind her voice,
a Liszt tarantella spins up toward
crescendo, the notes themselves revealing
how the body inside her body
has turned from her and started
to walk, the flux and dervish of cells
wearing her like a glove, stretching
the almost translucency of her being
which will, we think, at any moment
snap. And so it is that her voice
on the phone hardens, clacking
like dice through that thousand-mile
wire. And I, in my certainty, wearing
the hat of stalwart sons, mutter yes. And yes.
Strange to think, but so it is,
that the season my mother's life
begins to wane, whittled, moon-like
into startled, dwindling shards, is the season,
ten years gone, my father reached
for his own beaten heart. Reached and missed.

Snow on the ground. The air clamped
with cold. And I like to think that as she talks,
the creatures of home begin to appear,
those sentinels she calls sometimes
to tell me of: the blacksnake unfolding itself
in the high, hollowed-out bole on the trunk.
Or the great horned owl returned at last
to a lower branch, watching the hillside
for signs of its own life. Perhaps even
the fox will appear, burnt-red spirit of secrecy
and gifts, spirit of vanishing inside its own curve.
She watches as the words for her life edge
out of her, settling into the hieroglyphs of dying.
I can hear the fox's going in her eyes.

Red Fox, My Daughter

It is simple enough
the way I walk down to the river
to escape the heat, remove my shoes
and vanish a little while
into the dirty current.
It is simple enough the way
I sit out here on a rock,
shoes off, shirt off, watching skinks
flex their iridescent knees
up the not-quite-steaming rock walls.

Planes trace the river on their way
to or from the whitewashed city,
but they do not see the skinks,
they do not see the fish rising (whatever
fish can live in such a lake), to take
another insect—rings of water lapsing
into other, widening rings.

The sun turns a corner in the sky.
A crow heaves past, rattles
the black rasp in its throat.

It is simple enough
the way the red fox appears
on the farther bank, walking after hunger,
the way it paws a little in the sand,
rolling itself into the cooler earth.
I watch him from my rock, this
red apparition, this total being
who is not, after all, my daughter,

not a sign of longing or loss,
or even of beauty, though he is that.

I try to believe in the completeness of fox,
the particular shade of rust, the fox-like
scratch of an ear. The total attention
paid just now to an unremarkable sound
is the gift of fox-stillness, the perfect
forward-angling of his ears.
When he turns back to the woods
he turns back to the woods. Only that.

I pull on my shoes and clamber back up
to a stream of cold water, trees
thick with summer's final lull.
It is simple enough to walk like this,
to wherever it is I'm going,
thinking after the fox, my daughter,
grateful, if only, to know the world this way.

A Moment with Apples

It is rain again.
It is rain becoming
a mirror along
black stretches of road
winding through a country
that explodes
with the red of apples
at every turn.
It is rain glazing
the apples before they fall,
glazing the red glaze
of apples, which hang there,
silent, almost breathing,
feeling the change of
season move around
the shapes they make
in the unpronounceable air,
as if a pair of hands
moving that way,
almost touching, could
tell us something
we have no other way
of knowing.

Notes for a Poem about a Dream about My Daughter in which Moths Unexpectedly Appear

(for Anna)

First, the air: a snapped black sheet,
a constellation of bruised plums, cold
like the dull, undangered edge of a knife.
Next, the way the planet swings, rocking
in its tresses, a voice like water,
a mouth like a dish of kisses. Later,
after the weather shifts, clamps down, and
stays, my daughter comes in from the yard,
a white sack behind her trilling with moths—
thousands of orange-winged, red-tipped moths,
eye-spots like a world of vision.
I think for a minute of cottonwood leaves,
the underside of late-maple, or stemless
berries eddied up at the sharp turning of a creek.
I think how flowers can name themselves,
my mouth being shaped by *trillium, trillium, trillium.*
The laundry bag blooms like a breath, lifts,
and flurries open: and the room fills
with what wings are, my daughter
gleaming at the clever, whirling world,
her hands pulsing with in- and exhalations,
readying us all to be lifted.

Two

Triangulating Home

I have stared into the red sky
long enough, hauled
all the damnable weight
of the earth and all its orders
one time too many
to this cave my body
breathes from, and keeps.

I climb for hours out of the sun,
out of the earth-light,
climb for hours into
the cave-cold heights
of unlearning, into blue rain
blackening and blackening
all the broken bodies
laid out to forget themselves.

I reach back toward rock walls,
back to where the sun flamed
and seared the voices
from every stone, left them
mute and dumb and watching,
all of it unremembered.

I reach back to where the mulch is
cold and wet in my hands,
certain of no thing certain,
where my body builds and builds
itself over again, and over,
its planet still steaming, its eye
thick with lichen and clay,

where birds carry
the whole damned weight of the sky
balanced and nearly beautiful
across wings of unutterable wood.

The Carpenter

What I loved about my father
sawing wood on a Sunday afternoon
was the way he'd clench his teeth
in desperate concentration, the tip
of his tongue sticking out of
the bottom right corner of his mouth,
his whole face squinched
into a mound of misshapen certainty.
Mostly he did it from habit, some
rite of attention to the real and
ordinary, some devotional act
of mapping: muscle and wood and steel
triangulating a place where the world
might slow a little, the past ebb back
toward resiliency. He'd hold a length
of kiln-dried two-by-six up along the line
of his one unwavering eye, spinning it
like a circus prop, a long thin dancer in his hand.
Then he'd slap it down on the picnic bench,
bracing it with the ball of his four-toed foot
and the butt of his left hand. He'd
tease a notch into it, pulling up
on the blade one time, another time
pulling up, slowly, keeping a squinted eye
on the line he would coax across the grain.
Then he'd cut it up like kindling,
eight-inch lengths limbed off the original
body of wood, practice runs for the real work
of cobbling go-carts and stilts and shelves.

We'd sit and watch him, the yard full
of summer, sweet with the pulse of poplars
and dogwood—the summer hum of Maryland air
thick as wet paper. And the way his tongue
swelled red against the angle of his teeth
I kept thinking, he's going to bite it off,
he's going to bite his own tongue in two.
But those lengths of wood kept clattering
to the patio, swirling up the sawdust,
and my father, cocking his off-center eye at us,
would grin that safe-cracker's grin of his,
clicking and trilling his still-intact tongue
in delectable satisfaction.

Slicing Ginger

Not sex. Not sex,
but sexual: the way
the weather hangs
at the edges of sight,
the way the paring knife,
pressed and warm as any
lover to my hand, slides
just under the soaked
brown skin, opening
the earth of it, opening
the undiscovered, white-
fleshed seam in the scarred
and sacred earth: the
lemon-sweet, lemon-
sweet ringing of bodies
through the room.
Plumes of longing bleed
in my hand as the small
blade pares into the
mole-blind, uprooted,
incantatory fruit—the
slices hitting the
hot oiled iron with
a singing of fire on
wet wood, and the tiny
suns exploding there:
huge and redolent and
almost human.

Eight Months Married, Naked on the Couch,
They Watch the Academy Awards

The stars thank their own
luckiness, make
hard wishes for their own

lives flashing across
the flickering screen,
laugh and rise and teeter.

The husband's hand makes
circles over the wife's
breasts and stomach,

the wife's hand
obelisks and ovals
over the husband's.

No one told them
there could be a geometry
quite like this,

the angles their limbs
make during the long
spiraling-up of their love.

An actor, whose movie they
both had seen and liked,
thanks a friend and

colleague, a mother and a
wife, and holds the
familiar weight-lifter up,

Odyssean beauty, golden
in his fist, for a million
strangers to see.

The wife makes a joke
about prizes. The husband
starts to laugh and teeter,

and to rise. The applause
from the set makes the actor
grin, as it does

the performing husband
and wife, who wave
to the crowd, lost in the roles

and throes of their love.
Their delight is total
in all this delight, and

their joy for an award—
so many thanks, so many
kind people—they didn't

even know they were up for:
the luckiest days,
the sweetest delirium.

All Morning about Love

(for Susan)

I've tried to write
all morning about love,
a fable of this married life,
as though it were a trophy
won against glimmering odds
and what we ought to do
is hang it spotlit and shining
by the phone in the kitchen.
But I keep coming back to talk
of the season, the glissando of
rain coaxing the last few million
leaves from the last few thousand
limbs that still bear them.
I keep coming back to the sadder
adagio side of the world,
as though it were a hemispheric
thing, *my pitiful life in the*
Tropic of Sorrow (something like that).
But I turn and turn from this self-
indulgent whine, the way a season
turns (there it is again), the way
the light just now is turning
in the top of a spruce—
a blue spruce I notice when
I put my glasses on. So this
is a poem about love, a poem
of love, a love poem—why not
call it what it is? And when
I think of our married years

I think of what we have done
with our bodies, the flexing
and leaping, the staggering of
our human shapes which are
(as Whitman tells) all soul,
exalting in those brief
glimpses of heaven this separating
skin of ours cannot keep us
from reveling in, revealed.
And I think of the time we walked
by the river and you mentioned
the festival of flower-strewing
(Japanese or Jewish, I can't remember
which), wondering aloud
what the current would do
with all that blossoming.
Or the time we went to hear
the singing of Schubert songs,
and there in the middle of some
up-rushing splendor of notes, the
laughter came and came till we
snorted, the joy almost choking us.
It's a long way from the weekend
we camped high in the Rockies,
where the cougar circled our tent
all night, the silence of his
padding broken only by the
sonorous unearthly earthliness
of his growl—brought down, I thought,
by the scent of your monthly blood.

I stared so hard into the absolute
pitch of that lightlessness, I thought
something would give out (my fear,
its hunger), as you rolled back over
into your comfortable snore.
I hefted the twelve-D weight
of my boot—the only imagined weapon
at hand—and saw myself clubbing
that dangerous beauty as he sliced
through the tent to maul you like lunch.
I'd say a few words about the color
of the rocks in the river we followed
out of there, about the piping
of those tiny gray river pipers
we stopped an hour to watch in the
daylight's bright lull. But I
promised to stick to the matter at hand,
as though one of those rocks, one
of those piping pipers weren't part of it,
weren't even the whole resonant thing.
I know so little about it, love,
young as I am, stupid and inarticulate.
Rivers know much more. Rocks
the rivers gleam over know. I think
we should listen to what they say,
the names of the world caught and returned,
the way we'd listen to an old rabbi
rocking and muttering at his booth
on the corner, or even to some
drunk, rough-tweeded Irish sage,

careening on his bicycle down any
Wicklow hill. So I'll offer
great praise to the glory of maps,
the geography of bodies, the whole
terrain of listening. Praise
to the mapping and naming of all
these countries we invent as we go,
stumbling into them, crushed
and dazed with the local wine.
I hope you have a sense of what I mean
by this, of what I want to say.
There is more, of course—the night
we made love in the library,
slipping in and searching out
our favorite stacks—much more.
But it's getting late, the rain is
stopping, and I want to get this off to you.
I'll be back in a week, my basket
brimming with dried leaves,
wild to trace what the lamplight does
to the shadows on your collar-bone
and scapula and shoulder.

Poem for the Sleeper

Two crows land
on the twelfth-story
hammered-copper
cornice of a building
across the way,
and scrawk and
scratch their
stark, demented
dactyls into
the first teetering
hours of daylight.
They drop then,
pitching toward
the street, then
tuck, fold and bank
slightly west
to where the river
will take them
everywhere else.
Is it so strange
I write this
thinking of you,
a note for waking
a woman asleep
one room away,
curled against
this new breach
of February cold,
against the dreamt

shadows of crow-
wings pausing
over whatever
landscape your
dreaming furls and
unfurls you through?
The daylight shifts
a little, the twelfth-
story cornice hangs on
to its twelve-storied
corner of sky.
The winter light
shifts and trails off
in the trail of the
black flap of two
crows' uncertain drift—
thieves of gleaming
trinkets that they are.
So I am left in
their wake, which is
the wake of the visible
world and its story
of small, dubious facts.
It is the same world
you drift along,
more like a bird
in that tucked,
ancient pose than
anything a woman,

even winged, might be.
It is the same
precarious world
that resurrects itself
in the spaces
between your sleeping
and my waking breaths,
the same one we are
starting even now
to know—where gods
and lovers continue
to meet and nod and pass.

What Faith

It was one of those
singular New York scenes,
a man swirling madly
down the street, held
seemingly together
by the very rags
that seemed hell-bent
on tearing him apart.
He was weaving and
talking loudly to the air,
conducting with his
whole body a private
music, a symphony
that seemed from his
flow and ebb to be full
of waves or maybe
the wings of birds.
And there, in mid-block,
in mid-stride, in mid-
crescendo of whatever
rapture his being was
bent to, he dropped
to his knee exactly
in front of Our Lady
of Unutterable Faith
Church, bowed his head
and crossed himself
once, paused a brief
minute, and again
crossed himself.

And then he was up,
resuming his cadence,
flailing and calling out
his good mad passion.
And half a block
behind him, I wondered
what prayer it was
he offered, and to whom.
And I thought of course
of saintly Kit Smart
two centuries before,
dropping in the middle
of any London street,
and saying to the public
that might hear him
his prayers,
and to the daylight
that had blessed
and given them
his wild tirade of poems—
to the daylight he knew
to be full of God.

A City Letter to the Country

The fire trucks came again last night,
the stones of the city are burning.
And again the black wheels blow and crash,
weighted with the miles laid out
behind them, the litany of street names
naming themselves as they pass.

I want to try Alaska, the country's other
edge, where stars come down to rest
on the tundra, and people leave
gigantic piles of rocks on the snow
to be certain of wherever they've been.
I want to breathe myself back
into the quiet, to stare and ease my way
glacially through the days, and make
my living under so many hours of darkness.

In the firelight of another building
finally collapsed beneath this wrought iron sky,
I watch the cellists scavenging
for their songs, the poets dying of language
to say one thing exactly right.
On a distant rooftop, a woman folding
immaculate sheets stops to consider
all the constellations she knows are hers
and will never be able to name.

I want to ask directions for places
called for what they are: Snow-Light,
Weather-Home, Denali. I want to stand

at the center of the swirling globe, miles
from the city, and know for once the unwinding
of a place, the patiences and passions:
how a river willow is cut and bent to a snare,
how a marmot pads toward it—
the whole morning blue with precision.

Letter to Hugo from the Upper West Side

Dear Dick: Yesterday, my vision
blurring over grade-B headlines
and dirty magazines at a newsstand
run by a bleary, round Italian,
a man comes up out of the sudden
New York rain that works so hard
to give back into the air some
small part of this disappearing world,
and rasps at me, "I am a diabetic.
I need two dollars for some
shrimp fried rice." And something
about that lucky juxtaposition
of sentences and lucky rain
makes me think of you: the way poems
are uttered first by the world,
when we listen hard enough
and believe in luck. Fog
has settled hard over the Hudson
and rats are running there—
for their lives, I imagine,
the way we all are running
for (as in *in favor of*), our lives.
Since your death, Dick (and I hope
it's OK, me calling you Dick,
knowing you only by your poems),
I'm afraid the news isn't so good,
decimated lives and lands and such,
though a thousand poems have been
written, some of them beautiful,
whatever beautiful means, some of them

evocative as yours about Ten Sleep,
Upper Bumping, Skykomish—a few
of the names that take me back to places
like Savage Creek, where I watched
a thousand steep acres burn fast
as a held breath, the birds long-
flushed by the heat, the air
thrumming with fire, the fire
thrumming with brilliance and
a nearly devout kind of decimation.
Or the day I spent wandering
up the South Fork of the East Fork
of the Salmon River and walked
through a break of stunted white pine
into a herd of forty elk. The way
those huge heads lifted from the wet
alpine grass, and we stood there,
all of us, breathing steam, immobile
a very long minute, caught, the way
all of us are caught, between
the throes of astonishment and ruin.
It's November here, the month of blessings.
One of the twelve, as I'm starting
to learn. A good month for memory.
The sky is nearly white as paper,
written on and furiously erased.
There is nothing for it but to make
this letter into a dream you might
visit, or a poem you might nod over
over beers at some two-horse,

three-bar Montana town, before
walking out into the first morning
of a Montana winter, a day startled
with all the clarity of cold and light
this world of ours can muster:
elements that remind the body at last
of its first and final home.

Three

John Ruskin Considers the Nature of Water, Circa 1842

A found poem from Ruskin's Modern Painters

Now the fact is
that there is hardly
a roadside pond or pool
which has not as much
landscape *in* it as above it.
It is not the dull,
muddy, brown thing
we suppose it to be;
it has a heart like ourselves,
and in the bottom of that
there are the boughs
of the tall trees, and the
blades of the shaking grass,
and all manner of hues,
of variable, pleasant light
out of the sky; nay,
the ugly gutter that stagnates
over the drain bars,
in the heart of the foul city,
is not altogether base;
down in that, if you will look
deep enough, you may see
the dark, serious blue
of far-off sky, and the passing
of pure clouds.

Nightsong on the Salmon River

In the medallion light
of half a moon and aspen
flinching early to gold
the world is learning to die again.
Here, nine hundred miles from
salt air and tide pull, where
salmon climb through surges
of earth, breathing a final light
out, dying seems easy, resilient,
right. The night air chimes its
bell of ice. A nighthawk whirls,
taking an insect, shatters
the fragile air with vanishing.
And a seven-pound sockeye rises
to jewel the grayed gravel
in a fan of luminous eggs.
Like the salmon I have climbed
to this pool of thin water
to speak one sentence into the earth,
to learn to say one more way
of dying, the peculiar brilliance
of a thousand stars burning and
fading at the bottom of this alpine sea.
The firelight here joins any chorus,
snapping through the cadences of
pine, the applause of sparks starting
over water black and visible
as braille. The way it begins
the miraculous chanting, as
men and rocks have stooped here

through the nights, fingering the edges
of letting go and going on,
chanting through the solitudes
the sounds of early speech:
sockeye, sockeye. chinook, chinook.
coho, coho, coho.

Woodfire

Even dropped,
bucked, split and
set on fire, these
lengths of red oak
still make the season
sing—as the black
stove reddens,
clattering with heat,
as the heart of rings,
the good dry heart
lets go with the song
that all wood learns
when it is changed
to fire: release,
release. And the
forty-nine crows
that once cawed
after creation from
the wide, red splay
of the red oak's limbs
lift, two or three
at a time, from
another tree, the fire
still green in it.
It is the smoke
that takes them in,
its pale crow color
closes over their flying
and does not surprise

or change them, mute
or announce the
pitch of their desire
at all, at all, at all.

Essay on Empiricism

So this is how the possible occurs,
its body bent to the shape of a question:

A man wakes one morning into the cold,
dresses and walks away from his house

into the cold that he loves, into
a forest of oak, some high, straight pine,

tangles of rhododendron down the slope.
He can barely hear the sweeping

sound of his feet through the leaves,
or the muted bells of stream water

churling over the thousands-of-years-old rocks.
He is thinking of whole spans of his life

he would like to take back, a series
of months, and that year many years before

he would like to try over, like
a game whose rules he has only just fathomed—

there is so much to try and resay.
As he walks and thinks these things

to himself, he catches just a glimpse
of the unlit underside of huge wings passing

over the trees. And he thinks for a time
of that time at Hawk Mountain, how the

distance released wave after wave of hawks,
specks of flight that seemed to unvanish

out of the air: a thousand of them, someone
had said, more than a dozen species.

Is it possible that in the moment it takes
for his hand to curl over his squinting eyes,

for the thought of a longed-after life
to be replaced by the coming-into-focus of wings,

he is struck across the center of his back
by a trunk-thick limb of a tree that happens

to fall just then, just there? Is it possible
that his spine is shattered like a cord of ice,

that a lung collapses, that the right
side of his face is torn away by a rock edge

as he is splayed like a husk to the thick
decay of needles and leaves? Perhaps it happens

in slow motion: the touching of the branch almost
gentle on his shoulder, his body folding like

a rag, and the last break of breath breaking
out of him, unable to shape even a word.

It is like one of those Zen koans—an
answerless question that keeps the pupil filled

with emptiness as the possibilities spin:
What is the sound of one man dying? Or:

If a man dies in the forest and no one
is there to witness and to tell, what can be made

of his vanishing? Does a rill of his blood
color the leaves that don't stop falling?

Is this the shape of the possible: the un-
noticed dying of a man? The leaves that drop

from their places, as they will, and cover him
with their fading shapes? And the snow,

as it will, falls and covers him? And the
years, as they will, will him back into the dirt,

back into a lineage that is the earth's
alone, a veining of quartz through granite?

Has an hour passed since he started from home?
Two? Is it less? Some birds drift by—

swallows? swifts? It used to be so easy to tell—
And as they go, the front door of his house opens.

A woman steps out, his wife perhaps,
her arms wrapped across her body. She stands there

for several minutes, clutching herself and looking.
Cruelty is still some hours off. Longing. Sorrow.

She only thinks of the cold, how the clouds
are etched like iron against the sky—a beauty

she is only just learning to trust. Then she turns,
as she must, back to her life, a book to read,

the building shout of a kettle releasing steam.
All that she knows of the knowable world

remains—changed? unchanged? It hardly matters.
The latch of the door clicks to

in the perfect fit of the door frame: a sound
that is lost among other, less startling noises.

October Migration

Ice comes early to these fields
some years. The light narrows,
and a wind spills out over everything.

A woman steps out into it,
exchanges the long pull on her cigarette
for a lungful of autumn air,
leans in her long coat against
the frame of the farmhouse door
and watches the thunderheads build
and build half a state away.

Geese appear and she watches
their broken line turn east
then north, then east again.
She is thinking of smoke
winnowed out of chimneys,
apples piled or wheels of hay
scattered over open pasture.

She is thinking how the world
from up there really is a map,
how her body might float out
over it, following the folded
and refolded creases, the blue rivers
and brown roads easing and
coaxing her west and south and west again.

Every plod of the drifting cattle
is the last of the season.

Every fire-flash of the red-winged
blackbird is the last color
fleeing what becomes of the cold.

She is thinking of the staccatoed
ruckus the geese raise
in the last letter of flight
they write and rewrite across the sky.

It is a language she knows well,
a longing to sing hard above this
edged and fallow world, to move out
over the knotted distances
she has carried inside her
like rope for years.

Pilgrimage

I've never been to Jerusalem,
though I live near a synagogue
and have read a few times
the five books of Moses, a few
of the Prophets, even Ezra, even Job.
I've never been to Jerusalem,
though I've heard how the stones
of the wailing wall are mortared
with paper scraps and prayers.
I've never held the taste
of that sea in my mouth,
or known the clandestine scent
of jasmine and rifle smoke
mixing in the morning air.
I've never watched a woman carry
armloads of water over the dust,
bent and nodding under the weight of it,
as though it too were a child,
heavy as the dead–weight of water.
I've never been to Jerusalem,
though the Jews of my city
recite their beliefs, muttering
through the streets like all of us,
picking voices from the air,
lucky as fruit, saints that we are,
dazzled with all the madness of fathers.
When I make my way to the gates
of that city, I will set up my cart
of fruit and iced tea, and chant
like the east–side criers of my youth

the Hebrew names of berries and pears.
I will knock on the stones
long into the night, wild
with sadness, wild with joy,
teetering under all the gifts
my tired arms can bear.

Waiting for the Bus

Drunk again. Reading Baudelaire.
Reading Yeats who read Wordsworth
and thought all over again of home.
I am waiting for the bus to take me back
to where I'm going, to the mountains
or the coast, perhaps to the meadow
where the meadowlarks dramatize
their wounds, limping half-winged
through the sedge grass to draw
the predators away. There's a woman
standing in a half-lit doorway,
her hands in her pockets, her eyes
tracking the shadows on the street.
There's a man walking quickly
through the dust-filtered light, sorry
for what he does not know,
his mouth working on words he hopes
will be bright and dangerous as birds.
I am drunk again and making the day up as I go,
reading Neruda who is making love
to his wife, to the angle of light falling
across the shoulder of his wife, to the way
onions hump-up the soil in the garden,
a fruit so full of desire each has its own cosmology.
I am reading Clare, who is walking the pastureland
of Helpston, whistling back to the birds.
And Whitman. Of course I am reading Whitman,
who is walking home from a night at Pfaff's, flushed
with the fire of malt and local news.
Whatever he is thinking he is making love

to Neruda and John Clare, or would be,
were Isla Negra a little closer to Brooklyn,
or Brooklyn a farm in Northamptonshire.
The three great walkers, arms linked, are striding
through the waist-high grasses of Pennsylvania,
Essex, or the middle heights of the Andes,
singing rounds of drinking songs, stopping
for critter noise and the shadows of birds.
My daughters are at home, and it's a good day for dancing.
My wife's eyes will gleam with tears when she
walks in the door, telling me how the cellist in the subway
rocked to the pitch of Sixth Avenue, and of the deep,
resuscitating sadness of Brahms. It's a good day
for singing off-key, for making up words,
for really trying to see a piece of fruit.
From here the whole world bows as it passes,
and the bus, when it comes, will take me
everywhere I ever really wanted to go.

Four

Three Questions

How can it be
that the one sure thing
worth repeating
from a year that slips
between the hands
like kite string,
and is hauled into
the next like a
favorite kite,
is what I think is
a Japanese maple
from the far end
of November,
firing through half
a suburban block
with its not yet burnt–
through extravagance
of orange? Or that
that one tree on
that one block
seen on that one day
in the course of
this one short life
is enough, though clearly,
despite the lies
its leaves are, or
my need to trust
the impossible stories
hanging from its limbs,
it is enough? Or even
that the world, even

this one, can offer
so little and
so much at once
and mean them both?

Birds of Prayer

The story I hear is not the same
as the one I tell. That's how it is
with stories, though both this time have
birds all over their April-clustered branches.

Twilight Warbler. Ricochet Finch.

It is the season of migration,
which is the season of drifting, and of home,
which is the season the wind lifts us
back into whatever world we have lost
and names it over, which is forgiveness.

Dust-Sided Water Walker.
Colorado Flower-Sipper.
Air-Claimer. Pine Wielder.

My friend writes of the annual
Audubon Birdathon, tells of the species
he will pry from flight, reel in
with his dangerous, binoculared gaze:

Kansas-Backed Corn Thief.
Mississippi Fire Flapper.
Montana Tantalizer.
Idaho Spar-Sitter.
Seed Smasher. Dream Gleaner.

I would warn him of the hazards
of the magnified world, the day chiseled

clear through the eight-powered lens
until even its breathing is visible,
even its uneasiness, even its luck.

> *Eucharist Warbler.*
> *Silhouette Wren.*
> *Crayola Weather-Bill.*
> *Glint-Breasted Snowbird.*

Or the woman who would screech the car still
in eight lanes of traffic—semis piling
like cartoon trucks behind us—
for the chance to savor the late-autumn
passage of a line of birds of prayer.

> *Eastern Earth-Sifter.*
> *Western Meadow-Singer.*
> *Cinnamon Sleeper.*
> *Cowl-Headed Shadow Seizer.*

But who can account for the sadness
posed by the Gleam-Tipped Morning Mourner?
The recurring riddles called out
by a pair of Shining Idiot Questioners?

> *Dusk-Backed Gibbous Bird.*
> *Hurricane Healer.*
> *Bell-Throated Echoer.*
> *Nettleson's Sun Spotter.*

A Crescent Wren flashes through splays
of river willow. A Gray-Shinned Sand Gazer
shins and gazes over acres of sand.
Granite warblers are up from the south,
as is the Emery Rester and a solitary Zipper Finch.

Autumn Hopper. Lantern Walker.
Marsh Glider. Vinegar Tail.

How to dissuade the birder from birding
once the Muse Hatch has graced his vision?
The timidity of the Elm-Sided Rafter Wren,
or the Yellow-Crowned Drifter.

The skimmers will be out:

Lake-Sided, Dappled-Dazed,
Shadow-Backed and Eager.

If he's lucky, a Magnet Bird. If he's lucky,
a flock of Altitude Warblers.

Ivory Fluter. Water Stander.
Kiss-Breasted Maple Rester.

So I write back my wishes and hopes
and sighs—all the best for this world
of glimpses and half-heard song.

Dazzle-Backed Kinglet.
Glass-Winged Epiphany.

Though I can't quite help but remember the poet
who spoke into a blustering afternoon of wings:
You own the death of every bird you name.
And their lives? And the earth-bound shadows
that follow every wing-tilt? And the air
creased and mended with measures of flight?
Whose wonder are these to sing?

Air-Mender. Light-Dweller.
Clarity-Carrier.
Keener.

The Assassin

During what is still
so strangely called
the Great War, my
mother's father, a
medic for the father-
land, a flutist
of some repute, and a
reader even then
of Rilke's great sonnets,
pointed his rifle
at the air and squeezed.
A huge snowy owl—
so bright, he tried
to say, it became
a kind of incandescence—
dropped from a corner
of a nearby barn,
the bull's-eye of
owl blood broadening
over the feathers.
My grandfather still
tells this story almost
sixty years later.
We know him for music
and medicine, for
the birds he can
coax to his palm
with a seed, for the
chickadees he can
kiss a seed to, lips

and beak meeting
for one nearly endur-
able moment. To us
he is what kindness
is made of. And yet
he tells and tells
this story as though
it were a penance
he needed to get
just right, a myth
of beginnings
the elders share with
the gathered clan, or
as though he wanted us
to be standing there
with him, to see
the sweep of farm-
land drenched and
breathing, the
vineyards heavy with
fruit, and to feel—
even through
the thick gray wool
of army coat—the cold,
and to taste
the rifle-smoke taste
that clings even now
like flecks of iron
to the teeth.

Elegy for Zac

(for P.Z.L., 1975-1997)

Somewhere the sea is wrecking itself against
the jags and corrugations of the shore. But not here.

Somewhere a stone the size of a house slips off its millennial
mooring, a steep incline of mountainside that has held it in place

this age-long reach of ages, and thrashes its way
through talus and decimated patches of snow until gravity

gives it once more a place to rest. But not here.
Somewhere a man turns his head at an unexplainable noise;

a woman squints up from a book, taps two fingers on her knee,
goes back to the world on the page; somewhere a boy

walking a country road stoops for an old penny, flips it
once off his thumb like a planet, then shines it on his pants-leg,

grinning hugely for the gleam. But not here. Not here.
Here, a man wakes at the bottom of an empty well,

the ring of sunlight so far away, so faded and oblique,
he knows the world is over, he knows whatever world goes on out there

is not his world, the words for the things he knows not his words.
And he knows then that the poets have been wrong, that death,

as dominion, is a wing, a window, a way to reshape this
swirl of dust—that to conjugate the derivations of dying

is also a language of home, also a way of being, even by not being,
in the world. To curse, to bless, to say over and over

the name of a man who, with his going, leaves a space in the world
that words will never fill. Let our words be his words, our

bodies his body, let us shine these days until they gleam
and become, like a life, worth saving.

If This Were a Poem

There are three things I want to make clear from the very start:
First, the cobalt-bodied bodies of half a dozen dragonflies
drifting over the duckweed blooms at a lake,

a Wednesday afternoon, upstate New York, late May,
clear sky, a steel-like stillness, last year, maybe this.
Next, a young man, shirt off, unblazoned ball cap

pulled down for the sun—whose great, great uncle might
well have been one of Whitman's timid lovers for a time—
up on a suburban roof, his hammer-clenching hand

raised to that unconscious zenith that hammers love,
the good weight coming down, the calculus of force:
hammer to arm to body to roof to the rich red clay

of the earth spinning out and breathing, almost, breathing,
invisibly, invariably, northwest North Carolina, a Friday
in June, 1995, two hours before the thunderheads roll in.

And then, that one day, an Arizona August, the northeast
corner of the state, a small valley tucked away in a place
of pinnacled spires of rock, a world where time has,

more here than in other places, wrenched itself into
and out of the earth, given the world and taken it away
just like that, a late Sunday afternoon, bell-like weather,

a raven's-eye view of stark corrugations—a sudden upstream
gathering of rain slams into and slides off of the slick-edged
desert rock, forming, just like that, a wall of water,

which catches and folds over the unwary bodies of
twelve hikers, tangling them into the flashed moil
of silt-red water and uprooted cottonwoods, churning them

without a note of sadness or tragedy or grace through the
narrow sandstone canyon that water has carved away at
for upwards of thirty, even forty million years, and heaving them

one by one into the body of the lake miles below, where
the high sun no doubt seared them for hours and the vultures
circled no doubt and lowered themselves and circled some more.

If this were a poem it might well end the way it began,
with burnt-sienna dragonflies thrumming their transparent
acrobatics across the lake, pausing and repausing

over the twelve unstartling shapes the lake has started
to current out into its blue and then still bluer body.
Or with a man on top of a house stopping in mid hammer-swing

and turning toward what a voice on the radio is saying,
mopping his brow with his blue crumpled shirt and leaning
a little harder into the hot, half-shingled, steeply-pitched roof.

If this were a poem the world would be a different, deeper,
even more perceptive place: the cadences of loss, the syntax
of grief, the nomenclature of letting go and going on would

linger at the edge of the eye, at the space the hands curtail and keep,
at the point where the mouth shapes and is shaped by speech.
This is where breath becomes breathing, and breathing

a way to pause, to carry on, to pause. But this you know
is the news, days like all the days, stories to tell, riddles that hang
like half-focused photos of rain on the living room wall.

Take these, if you'll have them, for what they are.

Parable of Brother Sorrow

Because joy has wider wings
than sorrow, it disappears faster,
catching the first good thermal east,
sailing off into promises.
Sorrow meantime scrawks on its
leathery stubs, trying to gain on
altitude, kicking up rocks and dust
and the first dried leaves of October.
There is nothing for it but
to drain the fountains dry, pull
the suet from the trees, play Mahler
very loud. Even the dragonflies
stopped coming—long ago. That
should help. And the yellow jackets
have carried off the season's final
windfall. But sorrow remains
through all of it—the final
curtain its last laugh—starved
and glaring, almost Darwinian
this determined provider of absolutes.
So I strap on the prefab balsa
wings, the Daedalus & Sons logo
gleaming at each tip, and go out
to face this childish wretch,
this gloater who keeps the whole
neighborhood up with his dirges,
who will not quit these fenced-in yards,
these dying trees, the windrows and sandlots.
When I scrape the moss from his eyes
with a spoon, he is my son.

When I read a few of the more hopeful verses
from *Jubilate Agno,* he is my brother.
When I play the scratchiest of my
Danny Kaye records over and over,
and point to the western edge
of the world, and show him how
to work the wings, he is my lover,
and we remain in that place
of weeds and wilted dogwoods,
arching and flexing our backs,
thrumming and thrumming the air with
our good intentions and vanished hopes.
No one was surprised when sorrow moved in,
took my name, bore me a daughter.
No one was surprised when he started
teaching history at the public school—
an expert on famine and evolution.
The PTA embraced him, the Rotary and
Lions Clubs. He made millions at
bake sales, and never slept.
In a month he was sheriff; in six,
mayor. The lost son of Midas,
everything he touched turned to longing
and memory. The rest of it, the
burning of books, the banning of color,
the destruction of clocks, is forgettable.
He was gone for a month before anyone
noticed. His wings had grown wide
and black as a piano. He had slept
with every woman, every man.

He had eaten almost everything.
So the town held a meeting—it was
April and cold as nails. We rebuilt
the churches, planted pear trees
and acres of lilac. The days
were framed by matins and lauds.
When we spoke, we spoke in song,
and always in the future tense.
Every daughter was called Hope;
every son, Good-Luck. The streets
were renamed: Wishes Avenue,
Blessing Boulevard, Grace Street.
But the trees bore only the shadows
of fruit. The lilacs gave off
creosote and sulfur. The world became
irreparable and our own, pieced
together with all the remoteness
of living things. Years later,
joy was spotted just west of town,
tearing straw from the neck of a
scarecrow. Its wings had yellowed some,
and its song . . . its song . . . its song. . . .
No one could remember a single note.

Turning Over the Earth

Like Botticellian angels.
Like the huge blue angels of Chagall—

the way a raven looks up from the trace
of some creature into the middle of a

hot gravelly road, ruffles his iridescence
and makes for the one still branch of a pine.

Like the farmer leaning into the well-used shovel,
earth-colored now, the handle smoothed

with the human counterweight of dust,
the knowledge of furrows, postholes, and graves.

Like the graveyard workers in every corner
of every land, joking in every language about

the depth of holes, the power of rain
to work its way through, about roots and time

itself, about the fistful of black earth
they sift back down through soiled fingers.

It's two o'clock, and my mother
is troweling her tomato bed, breaking loose

clumps of sun-hardened clay, working
through the weeds in what we both know—

could we steel our mouths for the saying—
is her final summer on this ground.

She is half the age of the cottonwood
that shades half her yard, and the dirt

she turns, in a day or in a year, will settle
back down to its own right level. Shovel by

shovelful, she is turning over the earth.
It's four o'clock and my daughter is filling

a bucket with mud. A plastic spoon in one hand,
cup of water in the other—part Macbethian

witch, part Julia Child—she is realigning
the necessities of the earth, reweaving the world's

thick brew into what she says, with a grin, is lunch.
When she squeezes the muck between

her fingers, chortling as the black channels
calligraphy down her arms, the oozing becomes

the rhythm of rivers, a breeze stirring
the blossoms of lavender and ailanthus, of

blood and breathing, quartz veining through
mountains of granite. It's an old story,

the oldest, I suppose, how the gyre widens,
how rainwater runnels into rivers that fan out

into deltas wider than vision, how stars appear
to float in the perfect buoyancy of darkness.

Long-legged birds are there, lifting like gangly
angels out of the reeds and mudflats: ibis

and egret, cranes and night herons. A pair of
great blues rise like smoke on prehistoric wings.

And still, somehow, we find ourselves in this
one spot, reeking of loam and the salt of caves,

tethered like kites. Still, we learn the names of home,
we learn to drift, to dig in, to stay put, we learn to love

the quick trace of fire at the ends of our fingers.

Last Will

I am taking off the skin and draping it over
    the back of the chair.
I am unwinding the winding veins and hanging them
    from the branches outside.
I am whittling ribbons of flesh into the fish tank
    to feed the hungry fish.
And I am letting the blood spill out all over the floor
    so the floor shines back that thick mortal color.
I am putting the eyes in an egg-cup and the cup
    on the roof where the rain can fill it.
I am putting the knees in the hall closet, where they
    can pray in the darkness of old boots.
I am putting the feet in the bathtub for they are
    more like boats than feet.
And I am putting the cock and the hands together
    in the sock drawer, in their own good company.
I am putting the two round weights of the elbows
    on the desk where they belong.
I am putting the nose with the linen and all the lost odors
    of love and dying and long, connecting sleep.
And the ears I am putting by the door, where they
    might notice a key's click in the lock.
I am putting the hips and thighs and buttocks in
    a box in the attic with other old lamps.
And I am putting the mouth and lungs and the last
    held breath in the oven, and slamming the door.
I am putting the tongue on the window ledge where it
    can speak and taste and speak.
And I am unlocking all the locks of the bones and
    propping them up in all the corners of the house.

And I am going out, then, for a long walk
    by the river where I live,
In a morning too bright and resilient
    for this encumbering body to pass through
    and make it whole.

Acknowledgments

Grateful acknowledgment is made to the following publications, where these poems first appeared:

Carolina Quarterly: "A Moment with Apples"
"Nightsong on the Salmon River"

Chelsea: "Triangulating Home"
"Birds of Prayer"
"Letter to Hugo from the Upper West Side"
"Parable of Brother Sorrow"
"Last Will"

Columbia: A Magazine of Poetry & Prose: "Slicing Ginger"

Forpoetry.com: "All Morning about Love"
"Elegy for Zac"
"Notes for a Poem about a Dream
about My Daughter in which Moths
Unexpectedly Appear"
"Pilgrimage"

Georgia Review: "The Assassin"

Gettysburg Review: "The Muses of Farewell"

Heatherstone Poets & New Voices: Anniversary Edition:
"Three Questions"

Mid-American Review: "October Migration"

Orion: "Red Fox, My Daughter"

Poet Lore: "A City Letter to the Country"

Recorder: "Poem for the Sleeper"

My gratitude to the Corporation of Yaddo, for providing the crucial time and place for many of these poems. My thanks to Pattiann Rogers, for giving these poems a shove. And to Kevin Clark and Sharon Kraus, sustaining friends, unflagging readers.

Born and raised in Maryland, Ralph Black was educated at the University of Oregon and New York University. After college he worked for several years as a backcountry ranger and fire-fighter in the Sawtooth Mountains of central Idaho. His poems have appeared in such journals as the *Georgia Review*, the *Gettysburg Review, Orion,* and *Pequod* and have won awards from the Academy of American Poets as well as the *Chelsea* Poetry Prize. He has taught at NYU, Davidson College, and Wake Forest University. He is currently living with his wife and two daughters in County Wicklow, Ireland.

More Poetry from Milkweed Editions

To order books or for more information,
contact Milkweed at (800) 520-6455
or visit our website (www.milkweed.org).

Outsiders:
Poems about Rebels, Exiles, and Renegades
Edited by Laure-Anne Bosselaar

Urban Nature:
Poems about Wildlife in the City
Edited by Laure-Anne Bosselaar

Drive, They Said:
Poems about Americans and Their Cars
Edited by Kurt Brown

Verse and Universe:
Poems about Science and Mathematics
Edited by Kurt Brown

Night Out:
Poems about Hotels, Motels, Restaurants, and Bars
Edited by Kurt Brown and Laure-Anne Bosselaar

Astonishing World:
Selected Poems of Ángel González
Translated from the Spanish by Steven Ford Brown

Mixed Voices:
Contemporary Poems about Music
Edited by Emilie Buchwald and Ruth Roston

This Sporting Life:
Poems about Sports and Games
Edited by Emilie Buchwald and Ruth Roston

The Phoenix Gone, The Terrace Empty
Marilyn Chin

Twin Sons of Different Mirrors
Jack Driscoll and Bill Meissner

Invisible Horses
Patricia Goedicke

The Art of Writing:
Lu Chi's Wen Fu
Translated from the Chinese by Sam Hamill

Boxelder Bug Variations
Bill Holm

The Dead Get By with Everything
Bill Holm

Butterfly Effect
Harry Humes

The Freedom of History
Jim Moore

The Long Experience of Love
Jim Moore

Eating Bread and Honey
Pattiann Rogers

Firekeeper:
New and Selected Poems
Pattiann Rogers

White Flash / Black Rain:
Women of Japan Relive the Bomb
Edited by Lequita Vance-Watkins and Aratani Mariko

Milkweed Editions publishes with the intention of making a humane impact on society, in the belief that literature is a transformative art uniquely able to convey the essential experiences of the human heart and spirit. To that end, Milkweed publishes distinctive voices of literary merit in handsomely designed, visually dynamic books, exploring the ethical, cultural, and esthetic issues that free societies need continually to address. Milkweed Editions is a not-for-profit press.

Interior design by Wendy Holdman
Typeset in 11/15 Bembo
by Stanton Publication Services
Printed on acid-free 55# Glatfelter Writers paper
by Sheridan Books